SHOT DOWN

Glenn Cheney

SADDLEBACK
EDUCATIONAL PUBLISHING

ASTONISHING HEADLINES

Attacked

Captured

Condemned

Kidnapped

Lost and Found

Missing

Shot Down

Stowed Away

Stranded at Sea

Trapped

ISBN-13: 978-1-61651-924-7
ISBN-10: 1-61651-924-X
eBook: 978-1-61247-081-8

Printed in Malaysia

20 19 18 17 16   2 3 4 5 6

Photo Credits: Cover, AFP/Getty Images; page 28, Joe Bela, Getty; page 29, Copley News Service; page 57, C.E. Mitchell, BlackStar Photos; pages 68–69, William R. Crosby / Wirelmage / Getty Images; page 73, © Hubregt Visser | Dreamstime.com; pages 78–79, Bloomberg / Bloomberg / Getty Images, pages 86–87, AFP / ATTA KENARE / Getty Images

CONTENTS

It is every pilot's nightmare: getting hit by a missile or enemy bullets.

The attack usually comes from behind. An enemy fighter follows the plane, comes in close, and then shoots.

Sometimes the attack is a missile shot from the ground. Sometimes it is anti-aircraft fire.

Maybe the plane explodes. Maybe it just loses an engine. Maybe the pilot cannot control the plane. The plane is no longer a flying machine. It is a huge piece of metal falling to Earth. Just a little damage can cause any plane to crash.

But the pilot and crew can bail out of a warplane if it starts to go down. If the crew is lucky and quick, they will float to the earth by parachute.

Nobody can bail out of a passenger plane. If a missile hits a plane, it usually crashes, killing everyone on board.

Fighter pilots around the world have an agreement. They do not shoot down passenger planes. They only attack other warplanes.

But these rules are not always followed. Sometimes accidents do happen. In this book, you will read about planes that got shot down. Some were warplanes in times of war. Some were passenger planes in times of peace. Sometimes the people on board survived.

Sometimes they did not survive.

Ace Pilot Shot Down

DATAFILE

Timeline

December 1941

The United States declares war on Germany.

March 1944

Chuck Yeager's fighter plane is shot down over
Bordeaux, France.

Where is Bordeaux, France?

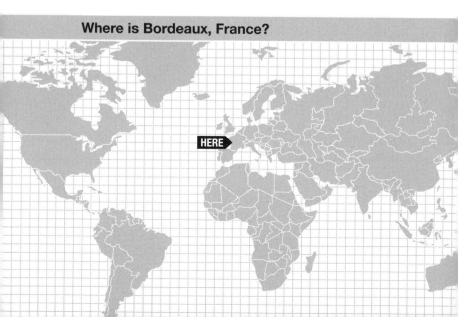

Key Terms

altitude—the vertical position of an object above the sea or land

cockpit—the front of the plane where the pilot sits and controls the plane

elevator—part of the small wing at the back of a plane used to make the plane go up or down

rudder—the part of a plane or boat used to steer it

?

Did You Know?

Germany attacked several countries in 1939 and 1940. In 1941, the United States joined England and France, and fought against Germany. At the same time, the United States also fought against Japan.

Ace Pilot Shot Down

On March 5, 1944, Chuck Yeager took off from England. His and three other P-51 fighter planes headed for Bordeaux, France.

Below them, World War II raged on. The German army had taken over France. Yeager's mission: To find German bombers at secret airfields in France and destroy them.

A Dangerous Mission

German fighter planes protected the airfields. They patrolled the skies, looking for American and English planes.

Yeager and the others flew in a diamond-shaped formation. Yeager flew in the rear—the most dangerous position. The German pilots usually attacked the plane in back first.

Yeager had a lot to watch out for. He had to stay with the other American planes. He had to look for bombers on the ground and for enemy fighter planes in the air. And he had to watch his plane's instruments and controls.

Hunting Planes

Yeager was a good pilot—quick, alert, brave, and smart. He had grown up in the mountains of West Virginia. He knew how to hunt. But now he was not hunting rabbits and squirrels. He was hunting enemy planes.

He was good at it. Yeager had already shot down two planes, and he had always flown home safely. But Yeager's luck was about to run out.

German Fighter Planes

Three German FW-190 fighters came swooping in from behind. Yeager saw the tracer bullet trails zip past his plane. He tried to dodge them, but it was too late.

As the bullets hit his plane, they cut its elevator cables. Yeager could not control the elevator wing at the back of the plane. He could not change his altitude.

To get away, Yeager used his rudder to do a snap roll. As the plane rolled to the side and spun upside down, the blood rushed to his head. Yeager escaped the attack, but he knew he would crash.

"I just got hit."

Pilots do not like to bail out of their planes. It is never easy and always dangerous. On a P-51, the pilot has to open the cockpit and climb out. It is not easy because the plane falls faster and faster, spinning as it goes. Yeager's heart pounded. He was scared, but he kept his cool. He radioed the other pilots and told them he was in trouble.

> *"I just got hit and have to bail out."*
> — *Chuck Yeager*

Yeager was three miles above the ground and falling fast!

Falling, Falling, Falling . . .

Yeager pulled open the cockpit. A powerful wind hit him in the face as the plane lurched downward. Yeager rolled into the air, and felt the sickening feeling of falling.

He was afraid to open his parachute too soon. It would slow him down, making him an easy target for the German pilots.

As he fell, Yeager ripped off his oxygen mask and helmet, and let them fly away. The rushing air ripped the breath from his lungs. It tore at his eyes and face. His flight suit flapped furiously. He fell fast, spinning as he went. When Yeager began to feel dizzy, he pulled his ripcord.

Yeager was very glad to see the chute open. It snapped him to an almost a dead stop in midair. The biggest danger had passed. Below him, his plane fell until it crashed to the ground. Yeager was glad he was not in it.

It felt good to drift gently below his parachute. But he was still 8,000 feet off the ground. Yeager was not safe yet.

An Easy Target

Yeager searched the ground for a safe place to land. He also searched the sky for his friends. And then he saw the enemy. A German FW-190 circled him and moved in to attack.

Hanging under his parachute, Yeager could do nothing. He slowly floated down, an easy target in a big sky.

Then he saw an American P-51 come in behind the enemy plane. The FW-190 took aim at Yeager and did not watch for other planes. The P-51 shot first, and the German plane exploded.

Yeager guided his parachute to a forest clearing. A small tree grew in the center. It snagged his parachute. Thinking fast, Yeager grabbed a branch. He released himself from the parachute, and the branch gently lowered him to the ground.

Saved by the French

Yeager was safely on the ground, but his parachute was still in the tree. It marked his location like a big, white flag. If the enemy found him, they would capture or kill him.

He buried his life preserver and started hiking. Yeager did not know which way to go. He just wanted to get away from the parachute. Before he went far, a few French people met him.

Yeager spoke no French. The French people spoke no English. They saw his uniform and understood he was American. They wanted to help him.

Danger for Everyone

The men took Yeager to an inn. The inn's owner warned him of the real danger. The Germans would kill him and anyone who helped him if he were discovered in France.

Yeager had to keep moving. For several days, he sneaked from house to house. Little by little he made his way to Spain. There were no Germans there.

In Spain, Yeager was safe, but he had no way to get home. He was stuck there with five other pilots. The president of Spain would not let them leave until the United States offered them something in return for their pilots.

Finally, the US government sent Spain a shipment of free gasoline. Spain sent the United States their six pilots. The boy from West Virginia was finally home.

Spy Plane Shot Down
DATAFILE

Timeline

February 1945

The Cold War begins.

May 1960

Francis Gary Powers is shot down in the Soviet Union.

December 1991

The Cold War ends.

Where is Sverdlovsk, Russia?

Key Terms

anti-aircraft missile—a missile that can shoot down a plane

CIA—Central Intelligence Agency; the American spy agency

telescopic lens—a powerful lens for seeing or magnifying the size of a distant object

U-2—a special spy plane

Did You Know?

For 40 years, the United States and the Soviet Union were in a "Cold War." It was not a war of guns, bombs, tanks, and soldiers. But each country was afraid the other was going to attack. They used spies to watch each other.

Spy Plane Shot Down

When Francis Gary Powers strapped himself into his U-2 spy plane on April 30, 1960, he thought it would be an easy mission. Powers would fly 3,700 miles over the Soviet Union on May 1st—a national holiday. His mission: To take pictures of a Soviet missile base.

Puppy 68 Away!

Powers' code name was "Puppy 68." As he took off from a base in Pakistan, a radio message went to Washington, DC. It said, "Puppy 68 is away!"

Powers did not know that a spy saw him take off. The Soviets knew he was coming.

He flew at 80,000 feet. Because of its long wings, the U-2 could fly higher than any other plane.

At that altitude, the air is very thin. There is very little oxygen. In a U-2, the pilot wears an oxygen mask. He also wears a heavy high altitude flight suit to keep him warm.

Dragon Lady

The U-2 was a secret aircraft. It had a nickname. It was called "Dragon Lady."

Powers liked flying his U-2. It was very quiet at such a high altitude, and very peaceful. He felt safe. No Soviet missiles or fighter jets could reach him—or so he thought. He was speeding along at 475 miles an hour.

A Pilot Alone

Powers flew alone. He could not use his radio during the secret mission, so there was no one to talk to. He also had to breathe through an oxygen mask the whole time.

Powers could see nothing on the ground. It was 15 miles underneath him! But the camera in the U-2 had a telescopic lens. It could take pictures of trucks, tanks, and missiles far below.

Powers thought about his family back in California. They did not know where he was. They did not know he was a spy.

An Orange Flash

Powers was 1,300 miles into Soviet territory when he saw a bright orange flash. He did not know what it was. Maybe it was lightning, he thought. Maybe it was a flash of the sun.

Powers did not know it, but the Soviets had shot 14 anti-aircraft missiles at him. One went high enough to explode near the U-2. It damaged the plane's tail.

Powers quickly checked his instruments. They did not show any problems. His plane seemed to fly normally. He was still at 80,000 feet.

But then he felt a change. The plane was sinking. It tipped forward a little, and then more.

Big Trouble

Powers' heart and brain raced. His instruments showed him losing altitude. He tried to raise the U-2's nose. It would not go up. He could not control the plane. He knew he was in trouble—big trouble.

He had to bail out!

The U-2 had one small bomb. But it was not for dropping on an enemy. It was to destroy the plane before it crashed. The CIA did not want the Soviet Union to capture the plane. It was full of secret equipment.

Bailing Out

Powers tried to eject out of the cockpit. A small explosion was supposed to throw him and his seat out of the plane.

It was not going to be fun. His plane was falling fast. When he ejected from the cockpit, 400-mile-per-hour winds would hit him.

At the same moment, his speed would drop from more than 400 miles per hour to almost nothing. The sudden stop would be like hitting a wall.

It could break bones.

Just before he ejected, Powers had to pull his legs from under the control panel. But they got stuck. If he ejected, his legs would be torn off.

To get his legs loose, he had to get out of his seat. But then he could not eject. He would have to open the cockpit, crawl out, and jump!

Powers loosened the cockpit roof. The wind ripped it away. A screaming cold wind tore at him. It was hard to move in his heavy flight suit.

He was just about to jump when he remembered the bomb.

Powers had to set off the bomb before he bailed out. He had to destroy the plane in the air. If he did not, the Soviets would find the camera. They would know he was a spy.

Bomb Switch

He reached for the switch to set off the bomb. It was a few inches too far. Powers tried harder, stretching as far as he could. The wind pulled at him like an angry monster.

Before he could reach the switch, Powers fell from the plane.

His parachute opened at 15,000 feet. As Powers drifted almost three miles to the ground, he saw his U-2 crash and explode below.

Powers landed near farms in an area called Sverdlovsk, Russia. The people were very surprised. First something exploded nearby. Then a man floated down from the sky.

Powers did not try to escape. He was unarmed and more than 1,300 miles from any other country. The Soviet police arrested him, but he did not tell them anything about his mission.

The U-2 was not completely destroyed. The Soviets pieced together the wreckage. They found the camera. They knew he was a spy!

Suicide Pin

Powers had a suicide pin tipped with poison. If he pricked his skin with it, he would die. It was for an emergency only. If he died, the Soviets could not force him to give them any secret information.

But Powers did not want to die. He had a family. He did not use the pin.

American Spy

The Soviet government said that Powers' spy plane proved that the United States was their enemy.

At first, President Eisenhower said that Powers was not a spy. He was only collecting information about the weather. He explained that Powers got lost and strayed into Soviet territory.

But the Soviets had pieces of the U-2. They had the camera. They showed the world that the U-2 was a spy plane. It was embarrassing for the United States.

Prison

The Soviets took Powers to Lubyanka prison in Moscow, the Soviet capital. They interrogated Powers for 61 days. For 10 to 16 hours a day, they hammered him with questions.

They asked him about his mission, his plane, and who sent him. Powers did not tell them any secrets. All he did was apologize.

The Soviets put Powers on trial and found him guilty of spying. Then they sentenced him to three years in prison and seven years of hard labor.

A Spy for a Spy

In June 1957, the United States captured Soviet spy Rudolf Abel. The CIA made a deal with the Soviet Union. They would trade a spy for a spy.

Powers came home on February 10, 1962. He never flew another spy mission.

Fifteen years later, Powers flew a traffic helicopter over Los Angeles. He gave traffic reports.

In 1977, the traffic helicopter crashed. Nobody shot it down. It had a mechanical problem. Francis Gary Powers died in the crash.

Two American Spy Planes

U-2

Nickname: Dragon Lady

Wingspan: 105 feet

Length: 63 feet

Height: 16 feet

Speed: 475 miles per hour

Maximum Altitude: 70,000+ feet

Crew: One

SR-71

Nickname: Blackbird

Wingspan: 55 feet

Length: 107 feet

Height: 18 feet

Speed: 2,000 miles per hour

Maximum Altitude: 85,000+ feet

Crew: Two

CHAPTER 3

Flight 007 Shot Down
DATAFILE

Timeline

January 1981
Ronald Reagan becomes president of the United States.

September 1983
The Soviet Union shoots down a Korean passenger plane.

Where is Sakhalin Island, Russia?

Key Terms

black boxes—well-protected recording devices used on airplanes to record what happens during a flight

garbled—confused or mixed up

off course—lost or not flying in the right direction

refuel—to get more fuel in the vehicle

Su-15—a Soviet Union fighter jet

Did You Know?

A black box is not black, it is bright orange. The bright color makes it easier for searchers to find it.

Flight 007 Shot Down

On September 1, 1983, a plane took off from New York City to South Korea. The plane was a Korean Airlines Boeing 747. It was a passenger plane called Flight 007.

Flight 007 carried 246 passengers and 23 crew members. The plane flew from New York to Alaska. There, it refueled for the long flight across the Pacific Ocean.

Flight 007 Off Course

For some reason, Flight 007 went off course. For several hours, Flight 007 flew in the wrong direction. It was still over the Pacific Ocean, but it flew toward the Soviet Union.

No one noticed that the plane was more than 200 miles off course. This was very unusual. Normally, passenger planes are tracked very carefully.

On that day, the Soviet Union would test a new missile. This was during the Cold War. The Soviet Union and the United States were enemies. They did not trust each other. They were both worried about spies and surprise attacks.

The Soviets worried when their radar showed a plane approaching. It was Flight 007. They thought it was a spy plane. It seemed as if it would fly over their military bases.

Flight 007 came closer and closer. It was still over the Pacific Ocean, but it was coming closer to the Soviet Union.

Most of the passengers were asleep. They did not expect any problems. They thought they were flying straight to South Korea.

Soviet Fighter Planes

As Flight 007 came closer and closer, the Soviets became more and more worried. They did not want an American spy plane over their country.

When the plane did not turn away, the Soviets sent two Su-15 fighter planes to meet it. When the pilots saw it, they knew it was a passenger plane. But was it full of passengers or spy equipment, such as cameras and listening devices?

The cabin lights were out as the passengers slept. The windows were dark.

The Su-15 fighter pilots called to the plane by radio. They told the pilot to turn his plane. The pilot did not answer.

Flight 007 flew over Sakhalin Island. The island was part of the Soviet Union. It was near a missile test site.

Shoot It Down!

The Soviet fighter pilots did not know what to do. They contacted their base. Their commander ordered them to shoot down the 747 if it did not leave Soviet airspace.

The Soviet fighter pilots flew in front of Flight 007. The plane did not turn. Again, they tried to contact Flight 007 by radio. There was no response.

One Su-15 fired cannon shots past Flight 007. It was a warning. The plane did not turn or change its altitude. All it did was slow down. But the pilots on board Flight 007 did not report anything unusual.

Two Missiles

Finally, one fighter pilot moved behind the passenger plane. He fired two missiles. Hitting such a large target was an easy shot. The missiles hit the plane. The plane did not explode, but it started to go down.

Out of control and flying in circles, Flight 007 went down. The passengers woke up. They did not know what was happening. They were scared and confused, screaming and holding each other. Some may have put on life preservers and prepared to crash.

As Flight 007 headed down, the pilots radioed for help. It was the only message that showed there was a problem. They never said anything about seeing the fighter planes.

After 12 terrifying minutes, the plane crashed. It hit the ocean near Sakhalin Island. A Japanese fisherman saw the explosion.

Black Boxes

Everyone was killed. But rescuers found only two bodies in the ocean. For six weeks, they looked for the two black boxes. They never found them.

The black boxes were a flight data recorder and a cockpit voice recorder. They contained information about the flight and what the crew said. This information could answer many questions.

Almost 10 years later, the Soviets gave the US government the missing black boxes. The Soviets had found them and kept them secret. One box was empty. The other box had garbled voice recordings.

Black Boxes

After a plane crash, everyone looks for the "black box." It is the most important part of the plane. And actually, there are two black boxes aboard passenger planes.

One is a flight data recorder. It records information about the flight. It records direction, altitude, weather, fuel levels, and problems with the plane.

The other is the cockpit voice recorder. It records everything the crew says in the cockpit.

If the plane crashes, the information in the black boxes may tell the cause. Investigators need to find them.

What should you do if you find a black box? Do not move it. Do not try to open it. Remember where it is. Call the police.

Unanswered Questions

Many people are still asking questions about Flight 007:

- Why did no one notice that the plane was off course?
- Why did the pilots fail to answer the Soviet radio calls?
- Why did the pilots fail to notice the Soviet fighter planes?
- Why were only two bodies found?

Secret Mission?

Some people believe Flight 007 was on a secret mission. Maybe the pilots knew, but the passengers did not know about it.

Today, the Cold War is over. But the true story of Flight 007 is still a mystery.

CHAPTER 4

Shot Down Over Iraq
DATAFILE

Timeline

March 2003
Operation Iraqi Freedom begins.

January 2004
Captain Kimberly Hampton's helicopter is shot
down over Fallujah, Iraq.

Where is Fallujah, Iraq?

HERE

Key Terms

attack helicopter—a helicopter that shoots at the enemy

erupt—to begin violently; to break out

invade—to enter an area in order to take it over by force

observation helicopter—a helicopter that watches for the enemy

zone—a specific area

?

Did You Know?

The United States invaded Afghanistan in 2002. The United States invaded Iraq in 2003. These invasions formed part of the US "War on Terror."

Shot Down Over Iraq

In January 2004, a battle erupted in the city of Fallujah, Iraq. Iraqi fighters battled American forces for the city.

It was a hard battle to fight. The enemy hid in houses and alleys. It was hard to see them. They did not wear uniforms. It was hard to know who was a fighter and who was not. The American soldiers needed help. They needed to know what was happening—where the enemy was hiding, or where they were shooting.

The military command sent Captain Kimberly Hampton and another pilot in a Kiowa observation helicopter to fly over the city. Their mission: To spot the enemy and report to the Americans on the ground. To the American soldiers, the Kiowa was like an angel in the sky.

Captain Kimberly Hampton was an excellent pilot. She had flown in battle zones in Afghanistan. She had also flown in South Korea.

Dark Horse Six

Back home in South Carolina, Kimberly's friends had always called her Kimbo. She was known for never losing a tennis match.

In Iraq, her helicopter code name was "Dark Horse Six." She was known for being smart and brave.

Dark Horse Six flew over the city. Captain Hampton kept the helicopter moving. She did not want to be an easy target. Captain Hampton studied the streets and alleys. When she saw people with weapons, she radioed the American troops. Sometimes she called in attack helicopters. They had machine guns, cannons, and missiles.

Flying in a war zone is dangerous, but Captain Hampton wanted to help the soldiers on the ground. She didn't want the enemy to attack them by surprise.

She kept moving around them, circling and changing altitude. Dark Horse Six was a hard target to hit.

Shot Down!

Suddenly a missile shot into the sky. It hit the Kiowa. The helicopter spun down, down, down. It did not explode, but it was out of control. It crashed to the ground near some American troops.

The Americans ran to help. Some helped the pilots while others guarded them against attack.

They could do nothing. Captain Kimberly Hampton was dead.

Three Medals

Captain Hampton was the first female American pilot to be killed in Iraq. She was also the first woman from South Carolina to die in Iraq. She was 27 years old when she died.

More than 1,200 people came to Kimberly's funeral. They wanted to say goodbye to the girl with the nice smile.

Captain Kimberly Hampton won three medals for her courage. At the funeral, the army gave her parents the medals.

The army sent soldiers and a horse to the funeral. It was a black horse with no rider—a horse for Dark Horse Six, Captain Kimberly Hampton. Or, as her friends knew her, Kimbo.

CHAPTER 5

Should We Shoot Down Passenger Planes?

DATAFILE

Timeline

September 2001
Terrorists hijack four passenger planes and crash them into three buildings and a field.

October 2001
The United States and other countries attack terrorist camps in Afghanistan.

Where is Washington, DC?

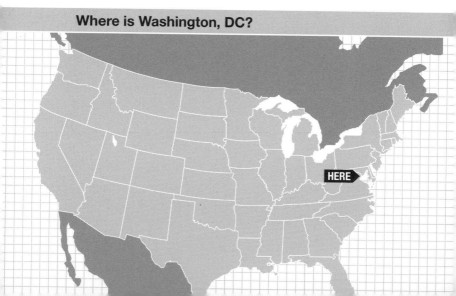

Key Terms

air marshal—an armed, undercover officer on a plane

depressurize—to lose pressure

hijack—to take over a plane by force

missile—a weapon thrown or projected so that it hits a target at a distance

target—something or someone fired at or marked for attack

Did You Know?

Missiles look for the heat of plane engines. But if the missile sees something hotter nearby, it goes there instead.

Should We Shoot Down Passenger Planes?

On September 11, 2001, terrorists hijacked four planes over the United States. The terrorists forced their way into the cockpits and took control of the planes.

In the hands of the terrorists, the planes were not just passenger planes. They were missiles— missiles full of people. They carried tons of fuel. They could destroy anything they hit.

The terrorists crashed two planes into the World Trade Center towers in New York. The Twin Towers were 110 stories high.

The planes exploded when they hit. The passengers were killed instantly. Many people in the buildings died in the explosions. Fires trapped other people in the towers.

Firefighters Rush In

Hundreds of firefighters rushed into the Twin Towers. They helped thousands of people get out, but they could not put out the fires.

In a short time, the buildings fell. Most people got out, but more than 2,700 did not get out alive.

That morning, the terrorists also flew a plane into the Pentagon in Washington, DC. The Pentagon is the home of the Department of Defense. More than 180 people died in the plane and the burning building.

The Fourth Plane

The passengers on the fourth plane heard what was happening in New York and DC. Some of their friends and families called them on cell phones. They told the passengers about the other planes.

Then the passengers knew what the terrorists were going to do. They knew they were going to die.

Fight for the Cockpit

The passengers decided to do something. They had to take control of the plane. Several brave passengers got up and attacked the cockpit door.

Nobody knows exactly what happened. There was probably a fight to get into the cockpit. Maybe the pilots died. Maybe passengers and terrorists fought over the controls.

The plane crashed in a field in Pennsylvania. No one knows why it crashed. Maybe the terrorists made it crash. Maybe the passengers forced it down during the struggle.

After the attacks, Americans were afraid of terrorists. No one knew what to expect. If terrorists hijacked another plane, what would they do with it? What would they hit?

Many Targets

America has many targets: skyscrapers, government buildings, bridges, military bases, nuclear power plants, and stadiums, just to name a few.

For example, if a plane hit a nuclear power plant, the effect would be terrible. Whole cities would have to be abandoned. Tens of thousands of people might die.

Ready for Take Off

Every day, across the country, fighter jets are now ready to take off. In 10 minutes, they can be in the air. A few minutes later, they can reach a hijacked plane.

The fighter pilots will do everything possible to avoid shooting down a plane. They'll try to contact the pilots by radio. They'll make sure the plane has been hijacked. They'll fire flares to warn the pilots. They'll fly near the plane and look into the cockpit.

The Final Order

At some point, the plane will no longer be considered a passenger plane. It will be considered a missile on its way to a target. To save other lives, the fighter pilots will shoot it down.

The fighter pilots will wait until the last minute. If they cannot force the plane to turn or to land, they will wait for the final order. If they receive that order, they will shoot the plane down.

During the September 11 attacks, President George W. Bush gave the air force a deadly order: Shoot down the hijacked planes heading toward Washington, DC. But the fighter pilots who scrambled to catch the planes never caught their targets.

It was a hard decision to make. Shooting down a passenger plane would kill hundreds of people.

Was it the Right Decision?

Many people think that President Bush made the right decision to issue this final order on the morning of September 11, 2001. Killing hundreds of people is bad. But letting terrorists kill thousands of people is worse.

Many others think it is wrong to shoot down a passenger plane. They remember the passengers on the plane over Pennsylvania. They think passengers can defend a plane.

"Shoot it down."

Everyone hopes it is never necessary to shoot down a passenger plane. But someday a fighter pilot might receive the final order: "Shoot it down."

- If you were the president, would you give the order?
- If you were a fighter pilot, would you obey the order?
- If you were a passenger or a pilot, how would you feel about the order?

Officials want to make that decision unnecessary. They want to keep terrorists off planes. Since September 11, the US government increased airport and airplane security.

Checkpoints

At the airport, only ticketed passengers can pass through the security checkpoint. They walk through a metal detector. Sometimes they are also searched. X-ray machines look into suitcases.

Passengers cannot carry things that can be used as weapons. They cannot carry knives, guns, scissors, box cutters, razors, or anything that is sharp. They can only carry a three ounce or smaller container of liquid or gel in their carry-ons.

In spite of the precautions, it is possible that someday terrorists will hijack another plane.

Air Marshals

In the United States, some planes have air marshals on board. They protect the plane if it is hijacked. The air marshals are armed. They are trained for this difficult and dangerous job.

Not all planes have air marshals. Terrorists never know if there is an air marshal on board. Air marshals wear plain clothes, not uniforms.

Protecting the Cockpit

Some pilots think they should be armed. They want to protect the cockpit. But others think pilots should not be armed. Pilots should fly their planes, not fight with terrorists.

A gun on a plane is very dangerous. At high altitude, a plane is packed with air, like a balloon.

One small bullet hole can make the plane depressurize. It might even explode. Also, a bullet could easily hit a passenger.

Maybe only air marshals should be armed. But not all planes have air marshals on board. If there is not an air marshal on board, then who is protecting the plane?

The crash sight of Flight 93 in Shanksville, Pennsylvania. The flight, bound for California, was hijacked by terrorists on September 11, 2001.

No-Fly Zones

Sometimes planes must stay out of certain areas. These areas are called "no-fly zones."

There was a no-fly zones over Washington, DC. in June 2004, at the funeral for former president Ronald Reagan. Many important people were at the funeral, including President Bush, Vice President Cheney, and the leaders of other countries. During the funeral, no planes could fly nearby.

During terrorism alerts, there are many no-fly zones around major cities and important sites.

No-Fly Zones Rules

- Pilots cannot circle or fly close to nuclear power plants.

- Planes must stay away from stadiums during baseball and football games.

- Planes cannot fly over military bases.

- Planes cannot fly over Camp David
  when the president is there.

- Planes cannot fly near the White House
  or the Vice President's house.

- During meetings of important officials,
  planes must stay away.

- On New Year's Eve, planes must stay at least
  five miles from Times Square
  in New York City.

CHAPTER 6

Navy SEAL Team 6
DATAFILE

Timeline

January 1944

The Naval Amphibious Base Coronado near San Diego, California, is commissioned for training and support of water- and land-based Navy units.

January 1962

Navy SEAL Teams 1 and 2 are established after President John F. Kennedy requests that a highly specialized warfare unit be created.

Where is Coronado, California?

HERE

Key Terms

amphibious—suited for both land and water

logistics—organization of moving, housing, and supplying troops and equipment

mission—an important assignment carried out for political, religious, or commercial purposes

seasoned—competent through trial and experience

Did You Know?

Naval Station Norfolk, in Norfolk, Virginia, houses the US Atlantic Fleet. The base is the home port for aircraft carriers, cruisers, destroyers, submarines, and a variety of other ships.

Navy SEAL Team 6

The US Navy SEALs are the toughest of the tough. And Team 6 is the toughest of the Navy SEALs. So when President Obama needed the toughest guys, he sent for Team 6. They are the special SEALs team that took out Osama bin Laden with two shots. He was Public Enemy Number One.

In one of their most famous missions, the SEALs landed in bin Laden's compound in Pakistan on May 1, 2011. The SEALs killed bin Laden and captured his family.

Team 6 was officially dissolved in 1987. Today the Navy calls them DEVGRU. That stands for the US Naval Special Warfare Development Group. But lots of people—and the media—still call them Team 6. That's a catchier name.

In fact, the Walt Disney Company tried to cash in on the name. It was the day after the Osama bin Laden raid. Disney attempted to trademark "SEAL Team 6." But they failed.

Team 6 was created in 1980. At that time, there were 52 American hostages in Iran. They had been captive there for more than a year. The hostages were held at the American Embassy in Tehran. Operation Eagle Claw failed to rescue them. Eight American servicemen were killed.

Not long after that, the hostages were released. But the hostage crisis led the government to realize that a team of special commandos was needed.

The Navy SEALs are commandos—soldiers trained to carry out special raids. They know how to sneak into enemy territory without getting caught. Once there, they do whatever is needed. If that means killing bad guys, that is what they do. SEALs take on difficult, dangerous missions.

Most SEALs are in their mid-thirties. That's about 10 years older than most sailors and soldiers. SEALs are seasoned fighters.

The word SEAL is short for SEa, Air, and Land. The SEALs are amphibious. Like frogs, they go from water to land and back. And they jump out of planes and helicopters in the air.

It's very hard to become a Navy SEAL. Every year about 1,000 men apply. But only about 200 to 250 make it.

SEALs have to be in extremely good physical shape. SEALs can easily do one-armed pushups and run for miles. But being tough is not enough. They also need to be smart, brave, and determined.

Most of the men who apply to become SEALs drop out. That's because the training is so hard. Navy SEAL training is not for the faint of heart. At least one recruit has died.

It takes nearly three years to fully train a Navy SEAL. During one of the first stages of training, the recruits have to go through "hell week." They get only about four hours of sleep in the five and a half days of hell week. They undergo physical conditioning for more than 20 hours a day. They run for 200 miles. They prove that they have the commitment and dedication to be SEALs. Guys who fail the training return to their regular Navy duties.

After the first phase, they learn scuba diving. That's diving underwater with air tanks. They get weapons training and learn about explosives. They learn how to parachute from a plane or helicopter. And they learn rappelling. That's when you slide rapidly down a rope.

There are other things they need to learn. Some SEALs learn a foreign language. For instance, the SEALs that killed bin Laden had to learn Arabic. They are also trained as medics. SEALs know how to save the life of someone injured.

SEALs also need to have excellent vision. They have to be able to shoot guns with extreme accuracy. Hitting the target is crucial. So is being able to decide in a split second whether or not to shoot. They also learn how to read maps and charts. That's so they can find their target.

Right now the Navy has a total of about 330,000 personnel. That includes officers and enlisted. The difference is that officers have been to college.

Some Navy people work on submarines. Others work on ships. Many work on aircraft carriers. Those are the huge ships that launch fighter airplanes. An aircraft carrier is like a small town. There are many different jobs for Navy personnel.

Out of the Navy's 330,000 people, only about 2,000 are SEALs. And out of those, only a few are on Team 6 (DEVGRU).

The team that killed bin Laden had 79 people on it. Out of those, only about 20 or so men took part in the raid. The others provided backup support and logistics. This includes providing transportation, computers, and weapons support.

Team 6 has done things like tracking down war criminals in Bosnia. They have fought bloody battles in Afghanistan. And they shot three Somali pirates who were holding an American hostage.

They have also tracked down international criminals like Manuel Noriega. Drug criminals like Pablo Escobar were SEAL targets too.

Before there were Navy SEALs, there were maritime commandos. Maritime means having to do with the oceans and other waterways. That's often how SEALs sneak in—by swimming.

US Navy SEALs rappel to the deck of the aircraft carrier USS *Enterprise* during an exercise.

The Amphibious Scout and Raider School was established in 1942. The Scouts and Raiders came from all branches of the military. They were the roots of the SEALs. They operated during World War II.

In the 1950s the Korean War came along. The Special Operations Group took on the role of maritime commandos.

In 1961 President Kennedy started the SEALs. That was during the Cold War. Cuba became a Communist country. It was only about 90 miles from US shores. So Americans felt threatened.

In a speech on May 25, 1961, Kennedy announced the plan to put a man on the moon. Everyone was excited about that. But he also said the government would spend $100 million on special forces, which includes the SEALs.

The first two SEAL teams were based in California and Virginia. Their first missions were in Cuba. They got into submarines and spied on the island. And they sneaked a CIA agent ashore. The agent took photos of Soviet nuclear missiles in Cuba.

Since then, the SEALs have been active in many areas. In the 1960s and 1970s it was Vietnam, Laos, and Cambodia. In the 1980s the SEALs were in Grenada. Later they were in the Middle East and Panama. In the 1990s they were involved in an operation in Somalia.

On August 6, 2011, a Chinook helicopter crashed in Afghanistan. It was shot down by a rocket-propelled grenade. The handheld rocket was fired by a Taliban terrorist. All 38 people aboard were killed. The dead included 22 Navy SEALs. Some were members of Team 6/DEVGRU. It was the worst loss of life so far during the Afghan war. Of the SEALs killed, none were involved in the bin Laden raid.

The worst SEAL disaster before that was also a Chinook helicopter crash. In Operation Red Wings, on June 28, 2005, 16 SEALs were killed. That helicopter was also shot down by the Taliban.

After the September 11, 2001, attacks, the SEALs swung into high gear. They became an antiterrorist group to be feared.

Today they continue fighting to keep Americans—and our allies—safe.

This military Chinook transport helicopter demonstrates a near vertical dive. A Chinook's troop capacity is 36 (33 troops plus 3 crew members).

Drones
DATAFILE

Timeline

February 26, 1973

The US military confirms to the US House Committee on Appropriations that they have been using unmanned aerial vehicles (UAV) in Vietnam.

February 2011

AeroVironment unveils the Nano Hummingbird UAV. It looks and behaves like a real hummingbird, but it is equipped with a small video camera.

Where is Iran?

Key Terms

CGI—computer-generated imagery

deploy—move (troops) into position for military action

drone—remote control mechanism, as a radio-controlled airplane or boat

GPS—Global Positioning System, an electronic system that uses satellites to determine the position of a vehicle, person, etc.

Did You Know?

The Predator drone is built by General Atomics based in San Diego. Each Predator costs between $4.5 million and $11 million. The world's deadliest drone, called the Reaper, is also built by General Atomics and costs $30 million.

Drones

You might want to think twice before you slap that mosquito. It could be an insect spy drone.

Researchers at Johns Hopkins University and Harvard are working on MAVs. That stands for micro aerial vehicles. However, the mosquito MAV is years away from reality.

But if it's ever built, this mosquito spy drone will look a lot like a real mosquito. It will fly like one, too. The size of an actual mosquito, it will fit on a fingertip. There is even a cgi-generated picture of one.

But this won't be any ordinary mosquito. The tiny flying robot will take photos. It will record conversations. It will land on your clothes—and follow you into your home. You won't even know it's there. And it will be remotely controlled. This means someone far away drives it.

Someday MAVs might even be able to get DNA samples. Just like a real mosquito, the MAV would suck a person's blood. Then it would fly back home to a lab. The blood would be DNA tested. The DNA test could prove whether or not the person is who they say they are.

Not all drones are tiny like MAVs. Some are the size of real airplanes. Between tiny and large drones, there are all sizes.

Drones come in all shapes, too. Some look like birds. Others look like planes or helicopters. But many drones look like something else altogether. It all depends on how they are used.

AeroVironment Inc.'s Nano Air Vehicle (NAV), also known as the Nano Hummingbird, is displayed. AeroViroment is developing the Nano Hummingbird under a research contract sponsored by the Defense Advanced Research Projects Agency (DARPA), an agency of the US Department of Defense.

With the war in Afghanistan slowing down, drone makers are looking for new markets. They are figuring out ways to use drones outside the military.

One way is for Hollywood movie producers to shoot video for Hollywood films. A small drone can fly into tiny places where a helicopter or airplane cannot. They are perfect for shooting footage for action movies.

There's a growing do-it-yourself drone movement too. People who are handy with building gadgets can learn to make their own drones.

Drones might even replace cars someday. Could you imagine getting to school in a drone? It could drop you off and fly back home to park. After school it could come get you. You could study, nap, or play video games as it flew you home.

Los Angeles area photographer Daniel Garate was using medium-size drones. He was using them to photograph luxury houses from the air. Then he sold the photos to real estate agents. The photos helped the real estate agents sell houses. Garate was making a good living at it.

Then the Los Angeles police shut him down. They told real estate agents not to buy photographs taken with drones. Using drones to make money was illegal.

That changed recently, however. In February 2012 the Federal Aviation Agency changed the law. They said it was okay to make money using drones. Daniel Garate and other drone photographers were back in business.

Image-capturing drones can be useful in other ways too. For instance, they can spot irrigation leaks in fields. This helps farmers.

Drones can be very expensive—millions of dollars. This is especially true of military drones. But others are affordable. Soon people will be able to buy a drone for only a few hundred dollars. And they'll be able to control it with their smart phone.

One cool flying drone is the Joggobot. Runners use it to keep an even pace. They tell the Joggobot how far and how fast they want to run. It flies along in front of them, about three feet off the ground. The runner wears a T-shirt with special symbols on it. The Joggobot uses the special symbols to help the jogger run at a steady pace.

Not all drones fly. The US Navy is working on an underwater drone. Called the Knifefish, the Navy's 19-foot-long underwater drone is good for finding mines. These underwater explosives can cause a lot of damage. They can blow up ships or cut communication cables. China has the world's largest supply of underwater mines.

There are some problems with underwater drones, though. Flying drones can be guided by satellites in the sky. Underwater drones cannot. The ocean floors are not flat. They are hilly in parts. In others, the ocean floor has deep ravines, or cracks. Also, the surface at the bottom keeps shifting. Underwater drones have a problem with running into things on the ocean floor. Still, they can tell a mine from a piece of rusty junk.

There are many other military uses for drones. They can be used for spying on enemies, and patrolling borders and restricted areas. Lives are saved when drones are used in warfare. And they can go into areas too dangerous for soldiers.

Many military drones are the size and shape of regular airplanes. These unmanned aircraft (UAs) have no pilot. They are controlled by computers.

New technology was created to help prevent drone crashes. This new kind of GPS system is called ADS-B. It sends a signal every second from the drone. It tells air traffic controllers exactly where a drone is. That way the drone won't crash into airliners or other planes.

Still, a drone crashes once in a while. In June 2012, a Navy drone crashed in Maryland. The unmanned aircraft crashed into a marsh. No one was injured. Luckily the crash was not in a populated area.

The US military uses drones to fight terrorists. In September 2011, a CIA drone killed Anwar al-Awlaki in Yemen. He was a top al-Qaeda terrorist.

The armed drone flew out of a US base on the Arabian Peninsula. It flew into Yemen and fired Hellfire missiles at a car with Awlaki in it.

In June 2012, another drone targeted Abu Yahya al-Libi. He was the new al-Qaeda leader after bin Laden was killed. The CIA's drone program has killed over 2,000 terrorists in the last eight years. That includes al-Qaeda, Taliban, and others.

Using drones is cheaper than deploying soldiers. It costs over $1 million per year for every soldier deployed to Afghanistan, for instance. That includes their equipment—tanks, guns, etc.

Many people are not sure if drones are a good idea. They say there are privacy concerns. Drones are very good at spying. People claim that they have seen flying robotic insects at political events. But no government agency admits to putting them out there. Yet US defense agencies paid for the research.

A captured US RQ-170 Sentinel drone went down in eastern Iran. Iranian officials were eager to exhibit a copy, which was on display next to the Azadi (Freedom) Tower

in Tehran, Iran, on February 11, 2012. The US insisted that it was highly unlikely that the Iranians were capable of building a functioning replica.

There is also concern about nuclear drones. Until recently, there was a problem with drones not being able to carry enough fuel. Drones could not fly too far without running out of fuel. For instance, the MQ-9 Reaper drone can fly for only 14 hours.

In July 2011, plans for a nuclear-powered drone were announced. Scientists at Sandia National Laboratories developed a nuclear drone that could fly for months.

However, the project was shelved. There was too much concern over what would happen if it crashed. Having a nuclear reactor aboard could be extremely dangerous. Officials decided it was too much of a risk.

Drones Are Big Business

American military contractors, like Northrop Grumman, are lobbying the US government to ease restrictions on exporting drones. There is a huge market for high-tech drones worldwide, with Israel and China leading in sales. Israel already sells drones to Azerbaijan, India, and Ecuador.

The US government argues that easing restrictions that have been in place since 1987 could lead to drones falling into enemy hands. Since there's no pilot at risk, people argue, drones could make it easier for governments to decide to go to war.

To get around the 1987 agreement banning the sale of large, pilotless aircraft, drone makers have been manufacturing smaller, lighter, unarmed versions. General Atomics, based in San Diego, has designed an unarmed version of its Predator in hopes of opening the export market.

It is estimated that the worldwide market for drone technology will double in the next decade. With the US continuing to build its drone fleet to around 7,500 aircraft, there's no doubt that other countries will not want to be left behind.

GLOSSARY

air marshal—an armed, undercover officer on a plane

altitude—the vertical position of an object above the sea or land

anti-aircraft missile—a missile that can shoot down a plane

attack helicopter—a helicopter that shoots at the enemy

black boxes—well-protected recording devices used on airplanes to record what happens during a flight

CGI—computer-generated imagery

CIA—(Central Intelligence Agency) the American spy agency

cockpit—the front of the plane where the pilot sits and controls the plane

deploy—move (troops) into position for military action

depressurize—to lose pressure

drone—remote control mechanism, as a radio-controlled airplane or boat

elevator—part of the small wing at the back of a plane used to make the plane go up or down

erupt—to begin violently; to break out

garbled—confused or mixed up

GPS—Global Positioning System, an electronic system that uses satellites to determine the position of a vehicle, person, etc.

hijack—to take over a plane by force

invade—to enter an area in order to take it over by force

missile—a weapon thrown or projected so that it hits a target at a distance

observation helicopter—a helicopter that watches for the enemy

off course—lost or not flying in the right direction

rudder—the part of a plane used to steer it

Su-15—a Soviet Union fighter jet

target—something or someone fired at or marked for attack

telescopic lens—a powerful lens for seeing or magnifying the size of a distant object

U-2—a special spy plane

zone—a specific area

Index